READER QUOTES

"Stanford Searl's poetry arises, as does an inspired message out of Quaker silence, from his daily faithfulness to the promptings of Spirit and a recognition that any moment may be sacramental, that Truth emerges from even the most mundane of experiences. Deeply informed by art, literature, history, his Quaker commitments, and a life well lived, Stanford's poetry is, itself, a source of inspiration – and enlightenment. The bonus is that it is also very enjoyable." (Max Carter, Director of Friends Center and Coordinator of Quaker Studies at Guilford College).

"From his perception of the `towering ocean of light' to an awareness of the rhythms underneath the silent surface,' Stan Searl here shares his own vivid experience of Quaker worship, set in a long history of testimony, felt in the heart of the individual, gathered in the group, `open to different noises/now harmonized' in the `odd dreaming' of those who `don't know what we're doing either/Leading with our noses/And smelling our way together.'" (Anne Dalke, member of Radnor Monthly Meeting, Villanova PA and Term Professor of English and Gender Studies, Bryn Mawr College)

"I love these poems. They are fresh and insightful and so delightfully Quaker. You have found a new voice, hallelujah!" (Ben Pink Dandelion, Professor of Quaker Studies, University of Birmingham).

"*This Quaker Woman* is my hoped for exit; the level of acceptance of death is very nicely put in these poems where you are with folks on their way out." (Ben Davis, Emeritus Professor, Union Institute & University).

D1428734

"Sometimes I wonder how you ever became a Quaker. You and silence seem like opposites. But that opposites attract so .... The poems are beautiful. They leave lots of pictures swirling around in my head." (Sarah Wickham Gicale, family friend).

"I identified strongly with `Car Wash Fantasy' in the ambivalence between simple expression and screaming out and publicizing our concerns and outraged feelings ... `The Bearded Clearness Committee' is brilliant – so often we want everything to be nice and work well, but we can't participate and do our part if we do not slow down and listen to the Light." (Dr. Joanna Komoska, Long Island Quaker and Family Therapist and certified Mediator).

"I must say that I find your poetry very accessible; that your love of Quakerism comes through strongly; and that the images and stories that you share speak poignantly to me." Steve Smith, Professor of Philosophy Emeritus, Claremont McKenna College, Clerk, Pacific Yearly Meeting and member, Claremont Monthly Meeting.

"I was deeply moved by Stanford Searl's collection, *Quaker Poems: The Heart Opened.* Stan's portrayals of the Spirit moving among Friends are simply and elegantly shared, throughout. His insights regarded Quaker history, worship and sensibilities are profound." (Donn Weinholtz, Ph.D., Director – Doctoral Program in Educational Leadership – University of Hartford and Co-Editor, *Quaker Higher Education*, an online publication of Friends Association of Higher Education and member, West Hartford Quaker Meeting.

QUAKER POEMS

The Heart Opened

STANFORD J. SEARL JR.
2014

ISBN: 1494489171
ISBN 13: 9781494489175

DEDICATION

For Rebecca Warren Searl

CONTENTS

PREFACE

A favorite memory of Stan Searl comes from the Friends Association for Higher Education conference at which Stan and I served together on a prayer committee, holding the conference and its work up in all the ways Friends of different branches do. Stan's prayer most often came as song, familiar hymns rumbling up his solid self and resonating as sound made Light. The poems in *Quaker Poems: The Heart Opened* likewise transmute the sounds of daily living and of song into the experience of Spirit.

Stan's many ways of knowing Quaker spiritual life—as scholar, as interviewer of many Friends about their own spiritual experiences, as teacher, as practicing Quaker, and as a person who has lived deep suffering and deeper love—inform these poems. Thus the book is divided into four groups of poems, each with a different emphasis. In the first section, the reader experiences Quaker worship, lingering with Stan and with other Friends, contemporary and historical. The poems of the second section reflect on Quaker history and bring us into the perspective of Friends such as George Fox, John Woolman, and Lucretia Mott. I think the brief "Activism and Outreach" section might be my favorite, as I am delighted to be surprised by the "Car Wash Fantasy" and the "Bearded Clearness Committee," among others. The book ends with "Quaker Values, People, and Themes," poems which let us live matters such as "Forgiveness," "Cancer Treatments," and "Worship Sharing" in the manner of Friends.

In *The Heart Opened*, Stan Searl's poems invite the reader into the experience of Quaker spirituality, from that of the gathered meeting, to a sense of living through the lives of Quakers before us and those around us, then shining out in daily life. Song and music recur as experience of and metaphor for spirit at work. With intensity in some poems, quiet reflection in others, and humor bubbling up throughout, the poems take the reader on the journey recapped in the final poem: from the disturbing violence of our contemporary world into the "stillness" and the "rhythm underneath the silent surface."

Barbara Dixson
Professor of English, University of Wisconsin Stevens Point and member of Stevens Point Monthly Meeting

I. Quaker Worship

A Quaker Poet

"Ashes! Ashes: We all fall down" (*Ring around the Rosie,* 17th century).

The thing is this:
I'm supposed to be a Quaker
And it has nothing to do with poetry.
After all,
One Quaker
Burned his violin
In 1675 on some London hill
Testifying about fleshy corruption.

Meanwhile,
As I center down in the opening of Quaker silent worship,
Hymn tunes
Come up out of memory,
Urging
Me to sing
And make a kind of music, if only inwardly.

Trouble is
That if I joined the 17th century Quaker
And burned up my instrument
I'd need to throw myself on a funeral pyre
And become ashes.

A POETICS OF SILENCE

All the talk about God irks me:
As I sit together with others in the Quaker worship,
Gathering silence and its breaths into my heart,
A new sense steals over me,
Murmuring sweet vibrations:
I float into a different breathing,
Transported underneath the surface into memory
Become an instrument upon which the Spirit may play.

Hymn tunes rumble though my body
Like Great is thy Faithfulness
Yet not so much the words themselves
But the tunes – inwardly and silently – pulsate through the chest cavity,
Breathing in,
Insistent,
Even though only heard as inward vibrations;
My body become a bass viol
Played upon in a new way.

"Breathe on me Breath of God" plays
Through my rising and falling chest,
As I sing first one part and then another,
Silently and inwardly
Yet the transport remains the same:
Mysteriously
Beneath the surface of the worship meeting,
The hymn plays within me,

Fills me with a new breath;
The tune drifts into the silent waiting of the worshipping group
To vibrate my body,
Touched and guided by the hymn as it
Penetrates through me.

THE GATHERED MEETING: PART 1

(for Cynthia Cuza)

It's like
Climbing Jacob's ladder
But
Upside down:
The ladder's
Straight,
Planted firmly
Yet
Leads
Down
Into the earth,
Opening
To luminous underground caves.

The movement
Slows
Like the adagio in Beethoven's
"Tempest" piano sonata,
Calm and
Harmonious,
Taking
Everyone in the silence
To
A lower level
Now
Drifting,
So many bass notes sounding
A pianissimo rumbling

Heard
Almost as words,
Some
Choir in the darkness
Leading
Everyone
Deeper
Into the mind's caves
And shadows
Offering glimpses
And an opening
To the beloved.

Near the bottom of this ladder
An expansive hand
Appears,
Open and
Wrinkled,
Etched deeply,
Dreaming as if we
Floated in the palm of an expanding hand,
Now
Encompassing the entire worship group,
Open to the
Hand's soft oils,
Soothing and
Sounding out
Rhythmic pulses from the deep
Singing out
Love,
Oh love,
How it grows
In the palm
Of the hand.

Mocking Birds and Quaker Meeting

This late January afternoon
I came back to our hilltop home in Culver City
And stopped
To listen to a mocking bird,
Full-throated
Singing
Its insistent song
Into the bright afternoon sunshine.

This morning,
Sitting on a bench in the Santa Monica Quaker worship,
I heard
Other warblings,
Throaty,
Perfectly modulated,
Yet coming from an underground place
Like the mockingbird,
As if the heart
Had become a taut string,
Vibrating,
Bringing songs home,
Deep and intense and true.

Listening,
Absorbed in the silence,
I heard a hymn tune
Over and over:
Spirit of the Living God

And realized that these Quaker speakers
Spawned together
From within the silence,
Bringing their hearts into the silent Presence,
Now become ministers
Urging one another on,
Opening themselves to the Spirit
Listening and
Proclaiming
The Spirit of the living God.

MUSING IN QUAKER WORSHIP

Musing about my Vermont grandmother
In the midst of Quaker silent worship,
I remembered
How she stood in the middle of our kitchen
Sipping her vodka and cranberry juice,
Bathed in the reflections from the afternoon light
From the Black River to the west,
The light
Twirled
Around her wispy white hair
As she became
Surrounded by streaming light beams
And she
Floated around the kitchen
In her own dance,
Murmuring
Oh it's so lovely,
So lovely
Leaking tears into the
Disappearing light
From the setting sun
Over the river,
My grandfather cooing
Oh Dickie,
Dickie,
My Dickie.

THE GATHERED MEETING: PART 2

"'Well, they call it a gathered Meeting where everyone who is there
is spiritually connected and the presence of God is real'" (Searl, *The
Meanings of Silence in Quaker Worship*).

The thing is
That sitting with all these other Quakers,
Open to the Spirit,
Listening,
Absorbed into the silent waiting,
Seemed
Like
Entering
Into a layered spider web
As if we
Vibrated together
Inside the worship space,
Gathered up into the
Throbbing
Undulations of a web,
Swaying
Together in some inner wind,
Pulsating together,
Entering
Sticky threads
Bound here,
Willing to be
Gathered into the web's center.

Drifting along in this resonant silence
I remembered
An orb-weaver spider
On the outside glass of our sliding kitchen door and
I noticed
Its eight eyes
Placed directly in the middle of the web,
Now
Buffeted by a swirling northwest
Flow around the hill.

In this quiet musing
The spider
Expanded,
Getting larger and larger,
Puffed up
Yet vibrating,
Hanging in the middle of the web
Swaying
To stiff, uneven winds and
Filling up the entire space
Outside the kitchen door
As Los Angeles shimmered
In the afternoon sun,
The entire sky
Fading
Into a purple sunset.

TODAY IN QUAKER WORSHIP

(for Tanna Moontaro)

Sitting together with everyone in the worship silence
I kept hearing hymns
And wondered:
What would happen if we all burst into song?
Would it come out
As those very Christian
19th century words
Praising Jesus
And asking for forgiveness
And reminding us how Christ died for our sins?

But today
It felt that to be open
And waiting on the Spirit
Meant something else.
I mean
When one Friend stood up to speak
We got the entire thing
Filtered through her voice
Chanting about
How we love one another
In the midst of our dying
Trying to remember how to be joyful.

This worship
Drives us deeper
Into the very silence
Where we started

As we wonder about a mystery
That flows through us
Speaking in other voices
Yet somehow like our own
Saying how much
We love one another even unto death.

SONG FOR WHITMAN

"I have no mockings or arguments, I witness and wait" (Walt Whitman, *Song of Myself*).

In the opening worship silence
Together with others,
I feel
Lines flow through me,
Entering
And pushing away all else,
Filling
My flesh and the appetites,
Pounding away in my chest
As I celebrate
These ruminating lines
As if they
Became
The only reality,
Thumping away
To accompany
The slow beating of my uneven heart muscle,
Pulsating now,
Sounding out floating lines in time
To my respiration and inspiration,
Singing together,
Oh Walt Whitman.

DEMETER'S RIPE CORN

Reflecting on Quaker silent worship's meanings,
I remembered sweet corn from Vermont's Westminister:
Driving home, taking up Route 91's gleanings,
I thought about my grandmother's ministry:

Walking into the Vermont kitchen,
Clutching huge, outsized ears of early summer corn
Seemed to lead into the depths of Demeter's riches,
Where she opened up her entire body to be born.

Even though my grandmother knew nothing about Quakers,
She stood at the center of the earth's passion,
Projecting an unresolved commitment to the body and its aching
As if some devouring appetite had overcome her World War II rations.

Even so, my grandfather and I sat in silent awe
At the joy of my grandmother's tasting and what we saw.

Wood Stoves and Quaker Worship

For one Quaker woman,
The hissing of the wood stove
Brought back childhood memories,
Projecting
Warmth and stillness
Into the room,
Reminding her of new shoes
And the gathering silence.

The wood stove
Crackled its way into stillness,
Now become
A pathway for memory
To wander
Its way into being,
Underneath the gathering worship silence,
Open to the heart's cracks
And leaking out heat
And light into the room.

THE GATHERED MEETING: PART 3

"Kiss me my father,/Touch me with your lips as I touch those I love,/
Breathe to me while I hold you close the secret of the murmuring I
envy" (Walt Whitman, "As I Ebb'd with the Ocean of Life").

Musing in the opening worship silence,
A murmuring entered me
As if the silent waiting
Gathered up
The sea's pebbles,
Surf
Pounding into the sand and
Churning out
Deafening waves
Carving into the sand,
Now
Booming
Curling up onto the salty, bubble-strewn beach,
Drawing the worshipping group
Underneath the surface,
Listening to the
Throbbing waves
Spitting out sand and debris
Over and over,
Bringing up sea-weed,
Slimy green tendrils from the deep,
Insistent
Pounding out this surf,
Filling up the silent bodies,
Booming out
Onto the sand,

Wave curling
Then falling back,
Sucking up white-capped water and
Sea-weed and shells
Rolling the worshippers together,
Mesmerized
By such oceanic energy,
Murmuring
Nothing and
Everything
Yet
Somehow representing a voice
And without a real voice,
Spilling waves
Into the silence itself,
Pushing
People together
Even though
Rolling
Thunderous churnings,
Open to different noises,
Now
Harmonized
Like a drunken Welsh miner's choir
Splayed out thousands of feet underground,
Reminded of the ocean's rumblings,
Insistent,
Charged into the underground
Of every soul,
Within the listening
Spirit of the worship silence and
The waves.

QUAKER STILLNESS

(for David Saunders)

       "Be still and know that I am God" (Psalm 46).
The stillness
Gathered,
Urging the two of us
To let go,
Opening to an odd dreaming
Both soothing and insistent,
The voice
Cooing,
Leading us
Over to the two Steinways in the Woodbrooke parlor:
As we touched the keyboards
Then descending,
An open-mouthed
Humming in our ears.
We listened together,
Allowing the octaves to resonate,
Organ-like from below,
The famous Steinway bass
Ringing out b-flat chords
As if from an organ stop,
Open-mouthed sounds from the deep.

A MEMORIAL MEETING FOR WORSHIP

(for Dora Stein)

Knowing you was like
Listening to a rock and roll song
Where the beat goes on
Beneath everything
Thumping and
Bumping,
Beating into our bodies
Pushing ourselves,
Singing and dancing
With the drums
Echoing
Onto our skins
Saying:
Look at me;
I'm
Alive the same as you.

After all,
As Quakers
We don't know what we're doing either
Leading with our noses
And smelling our way together.

Today
I dream of you
Sitting

On the couch
In your tiny Montana Street apartment,
Looking up at visitors
As if you had become illuminated,
Radiant,
The Inner Light
Spewing out its Truth into Santa Monica and
Flowing with you
Into the Pacific Ocean.

MUSING ABOUT PERSEPHONE

Yesterday,
Drifting into the Quaker worship,
I remembered how
My finger throbbed
As I picked up a branch
From the pomegranate bush out front,
A spiky thorn
Penetrated my right index finger,
Pushed through enough
To pulsate
Sticky red blood
Beating out onto the ground.

Those dark red pulsations of the blood
Remind me of Persephone,
How she
Throbbed next to Hades,
Trapped underground
By ingesting
Those blood red pomegranate seeds,
Juicy,
Now within her
As the bushes
Swayed back and forth,
The thorns
Small,
Yet spiky and sharp,
Buffeted
By the Santa Ana winds
Of the early evening.

Dreaming of Fanny Crosby

Sitting together with others in Quaker worship,
I recalled Fanny Crosby,
The prolific and blind 19th century hymn writer,
Sitting in her Manhattan apartment in October of 1863
And waiting for her musical collaborator,
Phoebe Knapp,
To arrive at Grand Central Station.

Fanny,
How did those words
Come flowing out of you?
Was it because
Jesus had entered your body,
Speaking through you
And how you felt
Touched
By his blood
To heal and redeem,
Throbbing inside of you?

Did it feel
Insistent
And wonderful,
Singing:
Oh Jesus,
Take me to your kingdom;
Give me your everlasting arms

And provide
Your blessed assurance
Oh great Jesus,
Right here and
Right now?

Song for Whittier

"Trembling, I listened: the summer sun/had the chill of snow ...."
(John Greenleaf Whittier, "Telling the Bees").

Today
I imagine
Those bees
And their hives
Draped with black mourning banners,
As I
Listen
To the local chore-girl in your poem,
Small yet
Alert,
Trembling and
Vibrating
Along with you and
The bees
Buzzing
Longing,
So peaceful with
Images of
Pastoral Massachusetts
As the boyhood farmstead
Comes into focus.

The desiccated rose bushes
Outside the homestead's kitchen door
Offer straggly blooms
Around to the edge of the garden terrace,
But

Everything
Leads over
To the bee hives,
Still draped with the shreds of black,
Taking us
Into a center of memory.

Listening
To a modulating tune from the bees,
I hear the
Chore-girl
Coo
Oh bees,
"Fly not hence!
Mistress Mary is dead and gone!"
I hear
A buzzing,
Sounding
Sweet changes,
Those pollen-loaded bees,
Heavy with early spring nectar and
Coming back home to the queen
Underneath the roses
Calling to you
Oh Whittier,
Come back
Home
To tell the bees
Keep there in the hives
Draped in black bunting
But
Ready
To pollinate

Out of the pink climbing roses
Again and again,
Insistent
With whirring and
Humming
To pollinate
Memory herself.

II. Quaker History

QUAKER ROOTS

(for Rebecca Warren Searl)

In the hot, humid morning,
Sweat dripping around the edges of her hair
And onto her forehead,
This Quaker woman
Seemed to hear a muffled voice from a long-dead Quaker ancestor
From the midst of the summertime graveyard
Behind Gwynedd Meetinghouse in Pennsylvania,
Saying:
Look to the ground beneath your feet
And feel the pulsations of these oak tree roots
Working their way up and out into this grave stone of your fifth great
grandfather
And listen to the inner music.

Walking into the early 19th century Gwynedd Meeting room,
With its wooden facing benches
And high, arched ceiling,
She sat underneath the circulating fans
And faced
Those other Quakers,
Both present and past,
Including one of the famous Quaker
D. Elton Trueblood's sons directly in front of her,
Listening to the voices
As if putting on a mystical earpiece,
Fitted just for this knowing,
Open to messages,

Become a testifying channel,
Proclaiming the Truth
And allowing everyone to see and feel and taste
The roots
And to bring the worshippers
Into communion.

Touched by
How the past and present
Happened right there,
It felt as if the oak tree's roots had thrust up into the center of worship,
Its sinewy sap
Filling up the room,
Poured into the worshippers
Like the whispers of the Divine Spirit's breath,
Testifying and
Proclaiming the Quaker tree of life.

HOMAGE TO GEORGE FOX

"And when all my hopes in them and in all men were gone, so that I
had nothing outwardly to help me, nor could tell what to do, then,
Oh then, I heard a voice which said, `There is one, even Christ Jesus,
that can speak to thy condition,' and when I heard it my heart did
leap for joy" (George Fox, *Journal*).

Last night
I dreamed of George Fox
Who stood next to Morecambe Bay's tidal flats on the Ulverston side
As a surge pushed in from the southwest,
Driven by stiff, gusty winds
To roil the flat, muddy water
So that the treacherous pathway through the quicksand
Disappeared in a churning salt spray.

The clouds
Scudded by
And the moon rose over the Bay,
Laying down a luminous shimmering:
I rode the moon's pathway into the past,
Slogging into muddy footsteps behind George Fox
As the misty, oily winter thickened and
Drew me into dreamlike contact with leather boots,
Smelly and fecund,
Following in the footsteps of Fox,
Walking now away from Morecambe Bay,
Turning back from the sharp, stinging salty puffs of wind

To make our way,
Albeit dreaming and
Riding the moon's pathway
To Swarthmore Hall.

A QUAKER HYMN

"Lord, I want to be a Christian in my heart"
(African-American Spiritual).

Lord
I want to be a Quaker
In my heart,
In my heart:
No more swearin'
No more chewin'
And no more smokin' either
And certainly no more liquor.
My people
What are you thinking about?

No more drinking,
No more meat;
No more killing and
No more violence and hatred,
No more goddamn war either:
What are you thinking about
My friends?

Lord
I want to be a Quaker
In my heart,
In my heart:
There's no more pollution,
Certainly no more wood fires in the fireplace,
My Friends
What are you thinking about?

There will be
No more polluting cars,
No more big oil companies,
No more military-industrial complex,
No more paying federal taxes for war,
No more military service
And no more American police-force to the world.
What about you thinking about
My Friends?

Besides
There will be
No more jealousy,
No more ego,
No more selfishness and
Certainly,
No more bragging
And self-congratulatory bullshit,
No more *me first* at all.
Lord
I want to be a Quaker
In my heart,
In my heart.

What are you thinking about
My people?

SWARTHMORE HALL

At Ulverston Steeple-house, Fox preached: "`You may say, Christ
saith this, and the Apostles say this; but what canst thou say?' This
opened me so, that it cut me to the Heart ..." (Margaret Fell,
Hidden in Plain Sight).

As I sat in the Quaker worship,
I felt silence
Gather,
Surrounding me,
Lifting me out of my chatty self
Into the past,
So
I entered into the world of George Fox
Sounding
The Day of the Lord at Swarthmore Hall.

George Fox
Spoke from
Underneath the silence
Asking questions
For which the priests
Had no answers:
And did the Lord your God
Speak to you,
Urging you
To follow him
To proclaim the Day of the Lord,
Going forth with a message
As from the prophets and apostles?

The priests
Turned over Fox
To the multitudes,
Who
Clawed and
Fell upon George Fox,
Beating him
With staves, fists and books,
Striking him all over,
Whipping him out of Ulverston,
Splitting open his head
As the blood
Poured out onto the ground.

Fox
Arose,
Saying:
"Strike again,
Here is my arms and
My head and
My cheeks."
Then
As Fox writes:
"And there was a mason,
A rude fellow,
Who gave me a blow with all his might just a-top my hand with his
rule-staff,
And my hand
And arm was so numbed and bruised
That I could not draw it unto me again.

And I looked at it in the love of God
And I was in the love of God
To them that had persecuted me" (George Fox, *Journal*).

Hymn for the Quaker Martyrs on Shelter Island

"Mary Dyer, Marmaduke Stevenson, William
Robinson and William Leddra who were
executed on Boston Common,
Of the suffering for conscience sake of
friends of Nathaniel Sylvester, most of whom
sought shelter here, including
George Fox, founder of the Society of
Quakers, and his followers."
(Inscribed on the Quaker cemetery monument at the Sylvester
Manor on Shelter Island, New York)

As we gathered in Quaker silent worship in the middle of a lovely sum-
mer morning
In the midst of woods at the edge of the Sylvester Manor
On Shelter Island,
An inch-worm
Loped its way along one of the log benches
Dangling its filaments over the edge
And pushing
Out its nearly invisible
Luminous threads
To prepare a pathway,
Creative
And open
Spinning out golden threads
As if the past really could become present
In a moment,
Illuminating the edges

Within the earth herself,
Felt as an opening
To the inch-worm's
Reeling in and out,
Undulating
Spinning threads from the tiny worm,
Trailing over to the granite monuments
Of the Quaker martyrs
Direct and true.

CRYING OUT AT LITCHFIELD

"When I came into a great field where there were shepherds keeping their sheep I was commanded of the Lord to pull off my shoes of a sudden; and I stood still, and the word of the Lord was like a fire in me ...." (George Fox, *Journal*).

They said he was crazy
And needed medication
Or electric shock
But
Sitting in the worship silence
I found myself on my feet
Crying out:
Woe onto the bloody city of Litchfield,
Following him out into the muddy winter fields;
Looking up at the two towers of Litchfield Cathedral
Fox became
Enraged
Like a bull,
Pulling off shoes,
Intoxicated with God's Word,
Swaggering through the fields,
Now walking barefoot and
Charging into the midst of the Litchfield market
Near the Cathedral,
Shouting,
Screaming out in the voice of the Divine
Oh woe to the bloody city of Litchfield,
Imagining how
Blood
Ran through the streets,

Crying out doom,
Striding through the city
With the two massive square towers of Litchfield Cathedral
Rearing up from the city center,
The feet getting colder and colder
Yet shouting
Woe unto the bloody city,
Crying out at market day
To call out to the Christian martyrs
Crucified hundreds of years before
Right there in the market square;
As if overcome by memory,
His voice flowed along the muddy tracks
Now saturated
By a dark reddish bloody mess
Making its way over the boots,
Pouring even into the Cathedral itself:
Oh woe
Unto the bloody city of Litchfield.

LISTENING TO THE BELLS

"'Repent, repent, woe, woe, the judge of the world has come.
Christ is in you all, believe not the priests of Baal, they are liars, they
delude you'" (H. Larry Ingle, *First Among Friends*).

Praying aloud for guidance
I found myself
Stumbling behind George Fox,
Listening to church bells
Ringing out chimes,
His rage
Possessed
Something out of Poe
As the bells sounded out through an inner ear
Booming out
The tintinnabulation of the bells,
Bells, bells,
Of the bells, bells, bells, bells.

As the bells
Pounded out,
Fox
Headed for the steeple-house
Feeling his rage
Spewing out
As if the reverberations of the bells
Challenged him
As he walked
To the church of St. Mary's in Nottingham,
Retching,
To speak out to the priest:

Oh you great idol,
Liar and cheat,
Selling Scripture for filth,
Woe unto you
Oh fallen priest,
Woe and beware
The Holy Spirit.

Fox stood
Proclaiming the Day of the Lord,
Moved by the Spirit
To thunder aloud
That God had come to teach his people himself.

People
Took hold of him,
Pushing him down underneath the back pew,
Beating on him
With Bibles and hymn books,
Grinding his head onto the
Cold stone floor
As they
Kicked at him,
Whacking away at his body,
Returning rage for rage
Behind the church pew at the back of the nave.

MUSING ABOUT JOHN WOOLMAN

"In this case I had a fresh confirmation that acting contrary to pres-
ent outward interest from a motive of divine love and in regard to
truth and righteousness, and thereby incurring the resentments of
people, opens the way to a treasure better than silver and to a friend-
ship exceeding the friendship of men"
(John Woolman, *Journal*).

The rain clouds
Obscured most of the Hollywood sign
As I mused in the afternoon,
Wondering
How to follow
John Woolman's Quaker threads
Left over in his journal.
So here
Prayer might be the first impulse
An opening
Into love in action,
Glimpses of Woolman's
Tenderness and
Love
Even for Quaker slave-holders
As he walked out into Maryland's eastern shore,
Exhausted,
Yet open to a divine love
Without any words at all,
Moving his frail body
To talk with these slave-holders

In tenderness and
Affection,
So low and humble that
Words
Became whispers
Sounding in his heart,
What with his un-dyed clothes,
Praying and
Paying for hospitality,
Refusing to write wills for slave-holders
Out of tender love and Truth.

May be
Access
Is by invitation only
To those who
Realize that
Love is the first motion?
Woolman's footsteps
Became clearer,
Leading to his
Humble exercise:
Love was his Ariadne,
Spinning out woolen threads
To walk in the Truth
As the Wool Man and tailor
Stiched up
His pants and shirts,
Laboring with weighty slave-holding Quakers
In love,
Not writing out their wills,
Urging others

To feel
The motions of divine love
In one's heart and
Renounce slavery.

John Woolman Walks out with the Delaware Indians in 1763

"And afterwards feeling my mind covered with the spirit of prayer, I told the interpreters that I found it in my heart to pray to God and believed if I prayed right he would hear me, and expressed my willingness for them to omit interpreting; so our meeting ended with a degree of divine love" (John Woolman, *Journal*).

Woolman
Felt
Divine love enter and
Fill him,
As he realized the
Wickedness and
Cheating of the
Frontier people for their own
Corruption and gain
As settlers
Stole
Delaware lands
Through rum and drunkenness,
Addicted to
Wealth and money;
Yet
He felt
Drawn
To a spirit of love and peace,
Open to more prayer and thanksgiving

Since
"Love is the first motion";
Woolman
Listened to the Delaware
To receive instructions
Even in the midst of frontier violence and murder
As he meditated
About the ironic success of the English,
Calling himself to more prayer,
To humility
As if he could become lower
Even as a worm,
Cleansing himself in Divine Love
To ripen his heart
So that greed and covetousness
Might be overcome.

In the midst of dangerous warfare,
Woolman and his Moravian companion
Had a meeting with the Delaware
On a June evening,
Divine love attending as well
But
The interpreters
Could not keep up
So
Woolman
Prayed,
Keeping an open channel to God
At the meeting,
Embedded in divine love over all;

He prayed that the Delaware would hear him,
Might feel his love for them,
Connected in the silent waiting between the words

To settle into the silence
After the English words
So that
Papunehang,
A chief of the Delaware,
Spoke briefly and
Woolman's interpreter said
The translation was thus:
"I love
To feel
Where words come from."

HYMN FOR LUCRETIA MOTT

"I would not weary you with words, fully believing that each
has a Teacher within himself; and obeying this, we need not
that any man should teach us" (Lucretia Mott, "Sermon to the
Medical Students," 1849).

You preached that
God has come now
To teach
How we should look to
The light of truth within.

I heard you
Singing
As you said
Privately and inwardly
Yet now sharing in Philadelphia
From 1849
To proclaim
Liberty
And its truth
Speaking in one's own heart,
Agitated
Yet urging
A faithfulness to the light
Now shining
As an advocate for the oppressed,
The poor,
The 3 million slaves,
The mentally ill,
The outcasts

To
Remember
Our father's love,
Etched upon the heart muscle as it
Breaks in upon the soul,
Celebrating
The father's love,
Listening
To the inward Teacher
As love
Fills up all
With a glorious joy.

CELEBRATING THOMAS KELLY

"For the heart of the religious life is in commitment and worship, not
in reflection and theory" (Thomas Kelly, *The Testament of Devotion*).

They say
Quakers
Believe anything and nothing
But
That's not true:
Kelly celebrated
A God-intoxicated life
In complete obedience
To the Divine call,
Abandoned to the moment,
The fruits
Ripening
Into
Humility and holiness,
Leading
Back into stillness,
Singing
Silent hymns
To a Divine presence
Who
Stole upon him,
Wiping out the self,
Wrapped up
Into the arms of the Divine.

The breath of God
Came sharp
Out of the northwest,
Blowing through the supplicant:
It opened in him
The power of love,
Which burst into song.

III. Activism and Outreach

CAR WASH FANTASY

(for Ann Fuller)

Sitting at the La Cienega
Car Wash in Los Angeles,
I watch the guy in a Dodgers baseball hat
Buff his rags over my Honda,
Opening up the trunk
Spraying and wiping away,
Noticing:
There's not a single bumper sticker or slogan
Or announcement
Or nothing
On the back of my car.

In fact
I don't even like to stick on those yearly DMV updates on the upper
right of my license plate
Because
I want the car
To be clean and perfect.
Yet
This afternoon at the car wash place,
Reading of the latest killings of American troops and others in
Afghanistan,
The worldwide terror reported in the newspaper lying in my lap,
I imagine
The entire Honda
Covered in antiwar signs, banners and announcement blasts

So that it's hard to see out of the back and side windows at all:
NO MORE WAR;
PEACE IS THE WAY;
MAKE LOVE NOT WAR
AND
BRING OUR TROOPS HOME NOW.

Sitting there,
Listening to the mourning doves,
I imagine
The pressure jets squirting out cleansing,
Purifying suds,
Overflowing
From the north end of the car wash,
Spilling out onto La Cienega itself,
Letting go an enormous rush of flushed out soap bubbles,
Flooding over
Where I'm sitting along the western edge of the building
As if pushed along by some underground force,
Roiling out onto the Boulevard,
Swallowing up the McDonald's across the side street,
Stopping traffic out there
As my own Honda
Floats along on the soapy surface,
Now turned into a neon billboard
That proclaims
PEACE IS THE ONLY WAY.

SINGING WITH LUCRETIA MOTT

"It is so simple, so beautiful, and I think so plainly in accordance
with His teaching – if they would not overlook this Spirit dwelling in
them" ("When the Heart is Attuned to Prayer," Brooklyn, New York,
November 24, 1867).

It's really annoying
To read your sermons and addresses
Because for you
It's all so simple:
God has come to teach us
Inwardly and directly;
The rest is all about fruits,
So that the ripeness is all.

You said
The great principles of justice and truth and love
Are
Imprinted onto our hearts
So
What's the problem?

We should
Cleave
To the everlasting
Divine truth of God in our hearts;
After all,
The Divine Spirit
Writes upon that muscle
Saying
Slavery is evil;

Resist it;
People are poor and dying;
Feed them
And give them shelter.

In accordance with your own teaching,
Proclaiming love and the
In-dwelling spirit and light,
The Divine Monitor
Emits
Love and peace,
Illustrating how
The government of God is within,
No teachers or authorities
Except for the
Truth of God's love
Written upon the
Fruits of the heart,
Pushing out the evil of slavery,
Pulling peace
Into the heart
Today.

GOATWALKING WITH JIM CORBETT

"From the time I turned Quaker, I've never reached a destination"
(Jim Corbett, *Goatwalking*).

Is this really poetry then,
These four-legged two-steps,
Goats in action,
Climbing up between rocks,
Rubble all-round them,
Sure-footed,
Hooves neatly alight
In a cliff-climbing dance
Like some odd 5/4 meter
Out of Dave Brubeck,
Wandering up and away
Into uncertainty?

Jim,
When you led those families from Guatemala and Mexico
Through the perils of the Sonora desert,
Did you share their life's warmth
And open
A desert spring for each one
Underneath the whole creation,
Eating and drinking together
In the unity of life and death
As Winstanley said,

Realizing
How the entire creation is knit together
Into a one-nesse of life?

Isn't this
A form of worship,
Meaning
How you
Entered
Into communion,
You and the immigrants
And the goats,
Holding onto one another
As if your lives
Depended on it?

After all,
Cowboy,
Park Ranger,
Teacher and
Goatwalker,
You brought hundreds of people home
To the source,
Embracing
Errantry as communion,
A witness
To wanderings,
Openings
And beginnings.

Oh goatwalker,
Crosser of boundaries,
Where does your spiky, goatlike beard point now,

Dreaming
Of these thorn-chewing,
Cliff-climbing hooves?

What might happen
If we followed you
Into the goat-infested wilderness,
Open to
A newly found
Desert spring
In our own lives?

THE BEARDED CLEARNESS
COMMITTEE

We met at a lovely park in Santa Monica,
The bearded clearness committee
Acting on behalf of the Santa Monica Quaker Meeting
To get
That damn white Van
Out of the Meeting's parking lot
Because
The neighbors
Didn't like it
How our homeless member
Pissed outside in our parking lot
And they threatened to call the cops.
As Grant started
To list the places where Nova could stay
I remember
How our member in need of clearness
Said
"Be quiet;
I want to talk."

I listened
In a lovely morning sun,
Warm and cozy
Even in mid-February and
I wondered:
What clearness
Could occur
By just listening to him?

But
I didn't care
Because
I had the two other bearded men
Who allowed me
To sit there on the bench,
Watching the nannies and their kids,
Only half-listening to the spew of words,
Looking out at other homeless men
Sprawled out on the spring grass
As if nobody had a care in the world
Except listening to the non-stop talking
About how
The boat sunk
In Marina Del Rey
And the Van
Stopped working
And how the son in Hawaii
Didn't seem to want him either.

Meanwhile
Sometime later
We got the white Van out of the parking lot
And
He found a half-way house near downtown Los Angeles
And
I picked him up
To drive him to the Quaker Meeting
But
Half-way to Santa Monica
I remember

Turning him
Saying:
I can't take anymore now;
Please
Be quiet
For a few minutes.

WALKING OUT WITH
HOWARD BRINTON

"As a great devotional writer tells us, only love can pierce the dark
cloud of unknowing" (Howard Brinton, *Friends for 300 Years*).

The afternoon wind
Picked up
Over the Santa Monica Mountains,
Pushing clouds down
Behind the Hollywood sign
As I sat
Reading
Howard Brinton's *Friends for 300 Years*,
Smelling the pages and
Imagining
Walking out with Brinton
Sixty years ago:
We strolled around
Pendle Hill, Pennsylvania,
Open to bird calls
Fluttering out in front of us,
Stooping
Over a large,
Blooming
Peace rose,
Its yellow flowers
Splashing
Open on this early September day.

Bending over the rose,
I start to fall
But
He caught me and
As I tried to steady myself,
A thorn
Spiked my left index finger,
A trail of blood
Dripping onto his book,
Leaving droplets of blood on the pages
Of the original 1952 edition,
An oozy sticky,
Deepening stain
Marking that volume.

Licking the blood from my finger,
I followed him
Into the Pendle Hill barn
For my first lesson about
The kernel of Quaker theology.

In the barn,
Cool and pure and sweet
Yet drowsy in the late afternoon sun,
We sat together
Knee to knee,
Waiting
And listening
In the afternoon silence,
Breathing together
As if open to a silent presence;
The Light
Stole upon us

And we became
Children of the Light,
Dwelling together
In God's presence.

Doing Good

The first great Commandment
Says
That we should
Love God
With all our hearts and minds and souls
And our neighbors
As ourselves.
That's it;
Period,
Beginning and the end
Wrapped up together.

I practiced
This preaching,
Helping to bring
A former Attica inmate
To Buffalo State College
Where I taught in the English Department.

Later,
I listened to the TV news
That this former Attica inmate
Killed
Two young female students just off-campus.

I wanted to flee
And bury my body
Into the rolling sand off Lake Erie,
Allowing
The powerful Niagara River

To float me down
Over the American Falls,
Feeling the mist and steam
From the roiling water
Crushing
My body
Forever.

THE WOUNDED HEALER

"'If we could read the secret history of our enemies, we should find
in each person's life sorrow and suffering enough to disarm all
hostility,'" from the poet, Longfellow (Gene Knudsen Hoffman,
Compassionate Listening, edited by Anthony Manousos).

This Quaker activist
Opened herself
To her own suffering and
To the mysteries of
Unhealed wounds in others,
Cleaving to
Thich Nhat Hanh's suggestions about violence:
He said that we should
Breathe on our anger and
Dislodge hatred and violence,
To follow in the footsteps of the Hiroshima Maidens,
Through which in their peace testimony
The terrible bomb
Burned out
Hatred and greed.

This compassionate listener
Tumbled over the side of her ship's journey,
Wallowing
Within waves of
Despair.
Even so
At the bottom of her tears,
Hearing nothing,
She touched

Great whales in the deep,
Now
Blowing out salty water,
Pushed upwards
Onto the surface
By the blow-hole of the Divine:
Briny water
Spilled out of her mouth and
Held her up above the surface,
Celebrating
That all life is God.

OPENING TO THE INNER TEACHER

"How is the Inward Teacher known? In joy and health, but also in loneliness and alienation; in the deepest encounters with other people and in dialogue with great ideas and works; in love but also in emptiness; in hunger but also in plenitude; in solitude but also in community" (Paul A. Lacey, *Education and the Inward Teacher*, Pendle Hill Pamphlet 278).

Outside my office window in Culver City,
The California laurel bush,
Laurus nobilis,
Spreads out above the white wooden railing
In the afternoon light,
A darker, deeper green
Than the avocado leaves
Behind it.
Covered with tiny late-January inedible berries,
These aromatic bay leaves
Provide a pathway
To the Inner Teacher,
Fecund and
Pungent in the warmish January air,
Shiny green leaves
Wafting
Astringently into the present.

These heart-shaped bay leaves,
Almost brittle,

Invite me
To follow
What Donald Hall
Called
A vatic voice,
All wrapped up
Within a wreathe of these shiny green- infused laurel leaves,
Opening to an Inner Teacher,
Become the blind seer Tiresias,
Yet low and humble,
Filling up
Teachers and students
Together,
Bay-infested,
Breaking open bay leaves
To cook together
A soulful,
Bay infused stew,
Crushing
The bay leaves together
To imbibe the Inner Teacher.

Poem for Shan Cretin and the American Friends Service Committee

Who knows
The mysteries of the human heart,
The odd pulsations,
From a young man
From Somalia,
Ending up in Kenya
Taught by
The American Friends Service Committee Quakers,
Open to
Alternatives to violence,
Rooting out
Anger and
Traveling in
As Douglas Steere,
Quaker writer said.

Isn't it
A wonderful thing
To celebrate
Peace and non-violence,
To listen to the inner truths
Of the other,
Watching and waiting

In the Light of God's Truth
To listen to
The heart's blood
Sloshing about,
Pumping out
Life
In the midst of suffering and trauma?

Thanks be to God
That in our dying,
We are in the midst of life,
Because
Those Burundi women,
Survivors of such terrors,
Family members
Cut to pieces
By friends and neighbors,
Remember
The source of love
In their hearts,
Holding one another,
Listening to the hearts'
Pumping
The light of God's infinite love
To overcome
Sin and darkness and
Evil.

WALKING TO PASADENA, CALIFORNIA

Looking at the edges of the San Gabriel Mountains to the northeast
Behind downtown Los Angeles
Some twenty miles away,
My mind
Drifted through the afternoon haze
To a grove of California Sycamores along the Arroyo Seco
On the way to Pasadena.

Newly married,
I imagined
How Quaker Anthony and his new wife, Jill,
Walked along the edges of a former creek
Amid the round and green flower clusters
And spiky fruits in the trees
As two red-tailed hawks floated in the updrafts.

As they made their way northeast
To that crown of the valley
Called Pasadena,
Thanks be to the great God
For such seeking together,
Walking through a Sycamore grove
On the way to Pasadena
Chanting,
Singing together

To raise up the poor and oppressed,
Brothers and sister in Christ,
Soaking up the Divine Spirit
As if it had
Seeped
Into their blood and bodies.

IV. Quaker Values, People and Themes

THIS QUAKER WOMAN

Never said a mean thing
About anyone in her life:
The world
Was wonderful
And
Even as she lay dying
And we listened
To her breathing shift
Into labored and
Rasping rhythms,
Her pulses
Ragged,
She offered up
A simple smile,
At peace and
Contented with her dying
As with her life,
Tranquil
And in love with the universe.

HOLDING HANDS IN
BEVERLY HILLS

As Quaker visitors,
We sat together
Outside a cave-like
One-bedroom apartment
Adjacent to Beverly Hills
Only a few blocks south of Sunset Boulevard.

As she requested,
I brought beer
To sooth her pain
And she opened
Two bottles of Anchor Steam
Before we left,
Saying
Oh it's so wonderful
I'm in such pain
Right here underneath
This breast.

We sat
In back of the apartment complex,
The three of us
Together in a gathering marine layer
Watching her
Pop
The two bottles
From an opener
Dangling from chains at her waist,

Listening to her
How the cancer
Seemed to
Burst out underneath her left breast,
Right here
She showed us,
Expanding,
Multiplying daily
Because
She had declined surgery, radiation, chemo and any morphine at all
Even when the
Hospice nurses
Pleaded with her
To take the morphine at least.

Before leaving,
We held hands
Murmuring how much we loved her.

A Quaker Dialogue

(for Elizabeth Cocca)

She said
Help me
To ring
The bells underneath the Eiffel Tower,
To toll out peace bells;
Ask John Williams
To harmonize these Paris Bells,
Ringing out
The blood of the cross.

I said
May the Catholic Holy Spirit
Find you
Underneath the earth,
To provide a
Pathway into your Pilgrim's heart
Rich in the blessings of the earth,
Heart-infused Quaker woman,
Catholic,
Insistent
Upon Jesus,
Open to love and to life.

Thank you
God
For this bell-clanging
Earth-insistent

Catholic Quaker woman,
Praying for peace and
Singing each noon
These hymns of innocence,
Harmonized by the Holy Spirit.

A QUAKER MUSICIAN

(for Rodney Pierce)

His instrument had become like an appendage,
Attached to him
And his heart
Now open to memory herself
Listening out in Eden, New York,
Standing in the midst of a grove of pine trees,
Remembering an up-bringing in Kansas,
Aware of the Bible's admonitions
To be low and humble and silent,
So that he
Heard then,
The cooing song of a wood thrush
Like an echo,
Just a little distant,
Always out in front
Yet
Sweeping into an inner ear,
Throbbing a music
As if joined with his oboe,
Practicing
Bird-like whistles
Yet underneath the surface
As from a cave
Inside himself,
Opening softly
To an underground of sound.

THOREAU'S BUSK AND
THE QUAKERS

"Would it not be well if we were to celebrate such a `busk,' or `feast
of first fruits,' as Bartram describes to have been the custom of the
Mucclasse Indians?" (Thoreau, *Walden*)

Thoreau
Said
The Mucclasse Indians
Believed the world
Ended every fifty years
And they
Celebrated by
Burning-up all their possessions,
Fasting and
Feasting
To start over again.

I wondered
What would happen if
This busk entered into my Quaker community
And became real:
Could we
Be born again
Out of the celebratory ashes,
Purified
Because
Breathed on
By the breath of God?

I prayed
That this renewal
Enter me,
Shaking off the old self
As if I
Had formerly possessed
A slick, mucous
Skin,
But no longer,
Sloughing off the old
Right here
And right now.

FORGIVENESS

Zeus speaks to Mnemosyne about their daughters, the Muses: "Each of our daughters shall be an *intermediary*, for she will lead the traveler on the best path" (Betty Mallet Smith, *The Greek Dialogues*).

Thank you
Job
For that faithfulness
In the midst
Of putrid sores,
An entire life
In shambles,
Disgusting
And in collapse.

I remember
"Though he slay me
Yet will I love him."
So
Even though
I don't have the
Holy Word in my hands
I thumb through memory
And she guides me,
Incising
The text onto my skin
And into my bones,
Filling me up and
Sweeping me
Into her arms.

LOVE POEM

"All you need is love" (The Beatles, 1967).

They say
Aphrodite
Came as a fair wind,
Daughter of earth's sweetness
Now
Blowing off the Pacific Ocean
Into your
Apartment in Marina Del Rey,
As you sat at the carved upright piano,
Hands on the keyboard,
Glancing up at one of Schumann's Scenes from Childhood,
The notes
Ringing out a sweet fragrance
Almost as if in a dream,
A whispering from the nearby sea
Entering into the apartment,
Singing from underneath the sorrows,
Penetrating the fingers
To flow into the heart,
Ringing out harmony,
Sounding
Again and again.

Meanwhile,
Hephaestus
Clanged along in his sea grotto,
Banging away
To make

His love a reality,
Shaping the rocks and stones themselves
To become
Playthings and poems,
Dancing
To underground tunes.

From those sea grottos underneath Mainra Del Rey,
Open
To love's music
That reached back into Manhattan's Island
And your imperious mother,
You insisted
That only love mattered,
Showing the way
Because
You loved them all
And that's enough.

Be not Afraid

(for Elfie Shuman)

I remember
Sitting with you
And other Quaker visitors
Outside Jim's hospital room
As he lay dying,
Thinking:
Thank you
God
For being here
With us in love,
Binding ourselves
Into one another.

It's as if Jung himself
Had appeared in the midst and
Took you by the hand,
Leading underneath the swirling waters of Quaker worship silence
To sing:
Be not afraid
For I am God
And suddenly
I felt your moist hand in mine
With nobody saying a thing.
We walked
Together,
Feeling the
Pulsations
In our clasped hands.

It felt
As if an undulating,
Rolling,
Curling wave
Had forced itself into the silence
And out of the depths:
We swam together
In a densely layered liquid of salted water
Like the Dead Sea itself
Sounding out from the depths,
Singing of love and
Death
And nothing at all.

CANCER TREATMENTS

(for Lee Storey)

I couldn't even get into the goddamn Condo,
What with the locked gate,
No key,
So
I stood around
Trying to fade into the bushes
Until
I could sneak in.
Besides
I didn't really know you
Before
We drove
Over to the
Lady of our Angels Hospital
For the chemo treatments.
Even so
When I drove you from Culver City,
We simply sat together anyway,
Looking out at the others in the chemo room,
Dying,
Shriveled skin
Yellow with the jaundice.

Besides
I loved going over to the Mexican place
Diagonal from the hospital

After we sat around,
Waiting for the chemo
To fill up your body.

Walking in
I stood at the counter
Looking at the menu in Spanish
And pointed to one of the signs
For meatball soup:
Hot and huge,
Ringed with bubbles,
Enormous meatballs
Floated
To the top of the broth.

On the way back to Culver City,
I wanted
To sing
But we were silent.

After the doctor said
That the tumors in the lungs and liver
Had only shrunk by 10%,
I cried
And we cried:
Coming back to the Condo
The afternoon sun
Poured into the living area
Now reaching to your mother
Who had come from Sedona, Arizona.

The two of you
Held hands:
As you sat back in the chair
Your mother said

How a presence appeared
Right there in the room,
Imagining a holy light
Surrounding you,
Seeming
To come out of the top of your head
You shimmered
In the midst of a bowl of light.

I prayed
For that healing energy
From Sedona
To lift your mother and you
Up into the afternoon light,
Overcoming and
Overreaching the 405 Freeway noises
Guided
By a power of love,
Even in the clear reality of death.

WITTGENSTEIN AND SILENCE

(for Newton Garver)

I remember
Cross-country skiing with you
Back in the woods around
The East Concord New York, home,
The snow
Puffy with light powder
As we
Cut through the evergreens.

After all,
In my early 30's
I could care less,
Challenging,
Fiercer every second
And sweating mightily
Even in the below zero temperature.

There we were:
Two Quakers,
Intensely spiritual,
Totally committed to silence
And its meanings,
Determined now
To beat the other,
To pummel the other one
Into the swirling snow drifts,
Curling around trees,
Overcome with hot desire.

In Wittgenstein,
What we cannot speak about,
The end of language and the beginning of understanding,
Is this ferocious competitive edge,
A way of being
That leads
To a bottom pool of silence,
Arguments and propositions be damned,
A truth that remains in the body
Just part of the breathing,
Pushing blood in and out,
The grammar and silence of Wittgenstein
Flowing and going together?

STANDING IN THE LIGHT WITH NEWTOWN, CONNECTICUT

December 14, 2012

"I saw also that there was an ocean of darkness and death, but an infinite ocean of light and love, which flowed over the ocean of darkness. And in that also I saw the infinite love of God; and I had great openings" (George Fox, *Journal*).

George Fox, the Quaker founder,
Stood
Amid sorrowing depression,
Open to blowing clouds,
Crying out the Day of the Lord
As he imagined
An ocean of light and love
Overcoming
An ocean of darkness in his heart,
Proclaiming
The Lord's presence over all.

May this
Flowing ocean of infinite light and love
Enter into so many broken hearts
To overcome
Satan's most recent disguise,
Wrapped up in black camouflage,
Killing
With his mother's guns
At Sandy Hook Elementary School.

Praise God
For this towering ocean of light:
May it
Swallow up evil
With its healing power and
Bring peace.

Worship Sharing with the Quakers

It's totally hopeless to be a Quaker today because
It's not about fighting,
Getting angry and swearing,
Calling people names and being totally pissed off
To want to kill the girlfriend and
Hitting her around the mouth and
Knocking out teeth and giving a bloody lip;
It's not about killing with fists, hammers, drones, rifles, hand-guns or
automatic weapons;
It's not about voices of rage or despair or suffering
To bleat out violence upon others or the self --
There's nothing like that at all:
It's all about silence and waiting and listening,
To become perfectly still
Like the statue of the martyred Mary Dyer on Boston Common
So that the hands are folded on one's lap and
The point is to be quiet,
Open to the Spirit and
Allowing entrance into one's heart and soul
As if released into a cloud of unknowing
To drift along with others,
Offering the stillness to enter from inside-out in order
To become someone else yet the same,
Breathing together with others and
Open to a rhythm underneath the silent surface
To allow the cloud to enter fully into the heart muscle,
Throbbing to some other beat.

ACKNOWLEDGEMENTS

Even though the poems were composed in 2012 and 2013, they really started about 1970, when I joined the Buffalo Monthly Meeting of the Religious Society of Friends. These poems reflect the inner travels of the heart, mind and soul, embedded in a wider Quaker community life. I stand in awe and wonder, musing upon the profound influences of belonging to and worshipping with the Buffalo, Syracuse and Peconic Bay, New York Friends' Meetings and finally, now, in my home Quaker Meeting in Southern California, the Santa Monica Monthly Meeting.

I wish to thank Quakers and other friends who became my built-in audience for some of these poems, particularly the Quaker women in our Light Group, including Cynthia Cuza, Rachel Fretz, Ann Fuller and Diane Manning as well as Shelley Blank, Elizabeth Cocca, Anita Hemphill and Don McCormick and Tanna Moontaro, all from the Santa Monica Monthly Meeting in California, as well as other Quakers, especially Anthony Manousos.

In particular, I wish to note Barbara Dixson's "Preface" to these poems as well as the reflections about the poems from Max Carter, Anne Dalke, Ben Pink Dandelion, Ben Davis, Sarah Wickham Gicale, Joanna Komoska, Steve Smith and Donn Weinholtz.

In addition, thanks to Cyrus Helf, Judith Searle and William Wallis for your technical and editorial gifts as well. Finally, thanks to my wife, Rebecca Warren Searl, for being such a key companion in this Quaker journey.

Stanford Searl, January, 2014

About the Author

Stanford J. Searl Jr. is a prolific writer and longtime follower of the Quaker faith. A member of the Santa Monica Monthly Meeting of the Religious Society of Friends, he currently lives in Culver City, California, with his wife, Rebecca, a birthright Quaker.

Searl holds a PhD in English from Syracuse University and previously worked as a core faculty member, mentor, and advisor at Union Institute & University, where, for nearly twenty-five years, he urged students to find and connect with their passion for learning and life.

Deciding to practice what he preached, Searl went on to pursue his own passions and completed qualitative research on Quaker silent worship, which led to his publication of two books on the topic, *Voices from the Silence* and *The Meanings of Silence in Quaker Worship*. His first book of poems, *Homage to the Lady with the Dirty Feet and other Vermont Poems*, was completed in 2013 and his second, *Quaker Poems: The Heart Opened*, shortly thereafter.

5983396R00077

Printed in Great Britain
by Amazon.co.uk, Ltd.,
Marston Gate.